American Moments

ABDO & Daughters

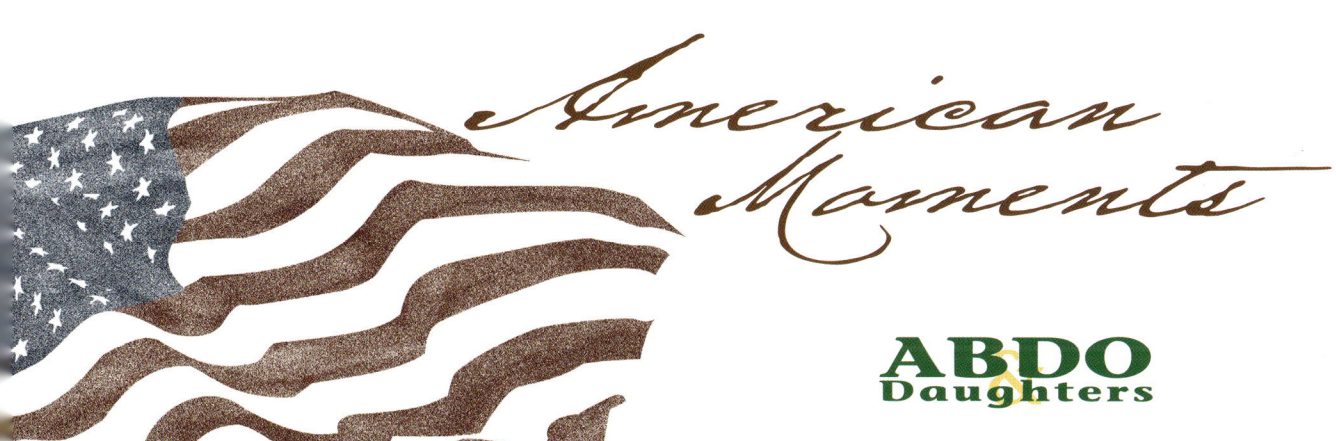

THE DRED SCOTT DECISION

By Cory Gunderson

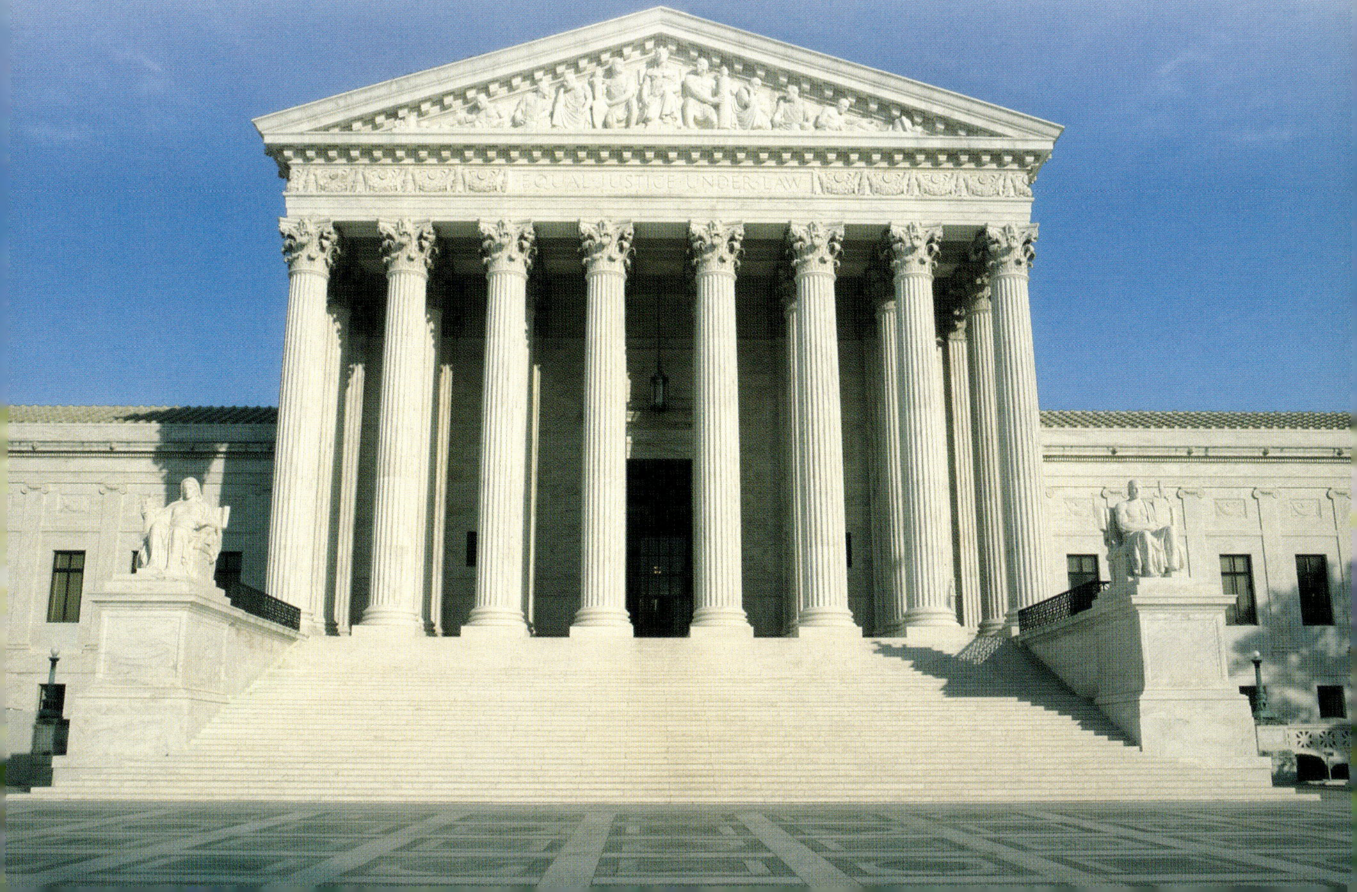

VISIT US AT
WWW.ABDOPUB.COM

Published by ABDO Publishing Company, 4940 Viking Drive, Suite 622, Edina, Minnesota 55435. Copyright ©2004 by Abdo Consulting Group, Inc. International copyrights reserved in all countries. No part of this book may be reproduced in any form without written permission from the publisher.

Printed in the United States.

Edited by: Alan Pierce
Contributing Editor: Kate A. Conley
Interior Production and Design: Terry Dunham Incorporated
Cover Design: Mighty Media
Photos: Corbis, Jefferson National Expansion Memorial/National Park Service, Library of Congress, Northwind

Library of Congress Cataloging-in-Publication Data

Gunderson, Cory Gideon.
  The Dred Scott decision / Cory Gunderson.
    p. cm. -- (American moments)
  Includes index.
  Summary: Details the various trials of the Dred Scott case and discusses its impact on the issue of slave rights in the context of United States politics and the Civil War.
  ISBN 1-59197-283-3
  1. Scott, Dred, 1809-1858--Trials, litigation, etc.--Juvenile literature. 2. Sanford, John F.A., 1806- or 7-1857--Trials, litigation, etc.--Juvenile literature. 3. Slavery--United States--Legal status of slaves in free states--Juvenile literature. 4. Slavery--Law and legislation--United States--History--Juvenile literature. [1. Scott, Dred, 1809-1858. 2. Slavery--Law and legislation.] I. Title. II Series.

KF228.27G86 2004
342.7308'7--dc22

2003058320

Contents

The Slavery Debate 4

Dred Scott, the Slave .14

The First Trial 18

The Second Trial 26

Federal Court 32

After the Supreme Court Decision 38

The Effect of Dred's Case 40

Timeline 42

Fast Facts 44

Web Sites 45

Glossary 46

Index 48

THE SLAVERY DEBATE

DRED SCOTT

Dred Scott was an African American who'd been born into slavery. In 1846, Dred and his wife, Harriet, asked the Missouri Circuit Court for the right to sue their owner for their freedom.

Dred's pursuit appeared straightforward when it began. For a number of years, he had lived with his master in a state and a territory where slavery was illegal. Other slaves in similar circumstances had won their freedom in earlier trials. But Dred's legal challenge lasted 11 years and became increasingly complex.

Dred's freedom suit evolved into such a controversy that it widened the gap between people living in the North and those living in the South. The outcome of his case contributed to the tension that caused some Southern slave states to leave the Union.

SLAVERY BEGINS IN AMERICA

In 1619, almost 200 years before Dred Scott's birth, the first Africans were brought to Jamestown, Virginia. Some were likely indentured servants. They worked for their masters for a specified number of years, after which they were freed. Others were slaves who were purchased by colonists.

A Dutch ship brings slaves to Jamestown, Virginia.

The Africans in bondage typically worked in tobacco fields. Tobacco grew well in Virginia, where land was plentiful and inexpensive. Tobacco farmers who had enough help to work the land could make large profits. By 1670, Virginia colonists were fully dependent upon slaves for their labor force.

By the early 1700s, African slaves worked in every American colony. As more slaves arrived, their working conditions became worse. The slaves came to be viewed as less than human, and they were often treated that way. Their masters fed them little but corn and pork and gave them used clothing to wear. Masters used whippings to train their slaves to be obedient and to work hard.

In the South, most citizens considered the right to own slaves no different than the right to own any other kind of property. In the North, attitudes toward slavery varied. Some people, such as the Quakers in Germantown, Pennsylvania, were very vocal in their protest of the practice. Their Christian beliefs led them to view ownership of another human being as immoral.

Other Northerners didn't give slavery much consideration. That's because the North's economy depended on slavery less than the South's economy did. Industries, which were much more prevalent in the North, could hire European immigrants at a low cost. And in the North, farms were smaller than those in the South. That meant Northern farmers could manage their land without the need for slaves.

In the South, however, large plantations were common. Many people were needed to work them. European immigrants often found the fieldwork too difficult, so they chose other occupations. The Southern economy relied on slavery to fill its need for workers. So great was the need for slavery that one farmer from South Carolina stated, "Slavery with us is no abstraction but a great and vital fact. Without it our every comfort would be taken from us. Our wives, our children made unhappy—education, the light of knowledge—all, all lost and our people lost forever."

Congress recognized the great difference between the Northern and Southern views on slavery. In 1787, Congress reached a compromise between its Northern and Southern members. This compromise was called the Northwest Ordinance. It prohibited slavery in the Northwest Territory.

The Northwest Territory had not yet been settled. It was made up of the land between the Ohio and Mississippi rivers north to the border between the United States and Canada. The Northwest Ordinance did not state the status of land south of the Ohio River. But, it was assumed that slavery would be legal there.

A cotton plantation in Georgia.

*****

Large cotton plantations emerged throughout the South. On these plantations, slaves who were field hands worked long hours to plant and harvest cotton. Men, women, and children worked in the fields. Plantation owners often hired an overseer, or supervisor, to exact as much work as possible from the slaves. In some cases, a slave might be expected to pick 300 pounds (136 kg) of cotton in a day. Slaves also had to endure physical punishments. Whippings were the most common form of punishment.

In the Northern states, slavery was gradually outlawed. By 1804, Connecticut, Massachusetts, New Hampshire, New Jersey, New York, Pennsylvania, and Rhode Island had been declared free states. These were considered the original free states. Delaware, Georgia, Maryland, North Carolina, South Carolina, and Virginia had been declared slave states. These Southern states were considered the original slave states.

SLAVERY SPREADS

By the 1790s, Southern farmers had hit hard times. The prices dropped for tobacco, indigo, and rice. They began to plant less. In turn, the need for slave labor lessened. It appeared as though slavery might end without a struggle between slave owners and those who opposed slavery. Slavery's quiet death, however, was not to be.

In 1793, Eli Whitney invented the cotton gin. Before Whitney's invention, seeds had to be removed by hand from cotton before it could be used. The cotton gin sped up this process. It cleaned 50 times more cotton per day than a worker could clean by hand. Cotton production soon increased dramatically and became very profitable. More people were needed to pick the cotton. Once again, slaves were in demand.

Eli Whitney's original cotton gin

The cotton gin wasn't the only factor in the spread of slavery. Beginning in 1803, the need for slaves increased even more. That year, the United States purchased territory west of the Mississippi River from the French. This transaction, called the Louisiana Purchase, doubled the country's size. As this territory was settled, more slaves were needed to work the land. Soon, decisions would have to be made as to whether new states in the West would be declared slave or free.

People quickly settled in the new territory. About 56,000 whites had settled in the Missouri Territory by 1819. The territory's population was now large enough to request statehood. Its request came at a time when the United States was comprised of 11 free states and 11 slave states. All of the congressmen were aware of this delicate balance. To tip it one way or the other would surely increase the friction between the North and the South.

For more than a year, members of Congress debated whether Missouri would be admitted as a free state or a slave state. Not surprisingly, Southern congressmen wanted Missouri to be admitted as a slave state. Northern congressmen, however, had hoped to prevent the spread of slavery in the United States.

Henry Clay

In 1820, Speaker of the House Henry Clay guided Congress to a compromise. This deal was called the Missouri Compromise of 1820. It admitted Missouri as a slave state. At the same time, it granted statehood to Maine, where slavery was forbidden. The compromise maintained the balance between free and slave states. There were now 12 of each.

The Missouri Compromise also created a new boundary. It was an imaginary line across the Louisiana Territory along the

12

southern border of Missouri. Slavery was banned north of this line except in Missouri. Slavery was allowed south of the line.

The Missouri Compromise quickly met criticism. Northerners were unhappy that slavery was allowed in Missouri. Southerners were angry that the federal government had the power to ban slavery from parts of the new territory. They believed that each state should decide the slavery issue for itself. Despite the criticism, the compromise temporarily settled the issue of slavery.

Within three decades after the Missouri Compromise, Dred Scott's legal plea for freedom began. His case and other events would open the slavery debate once again.

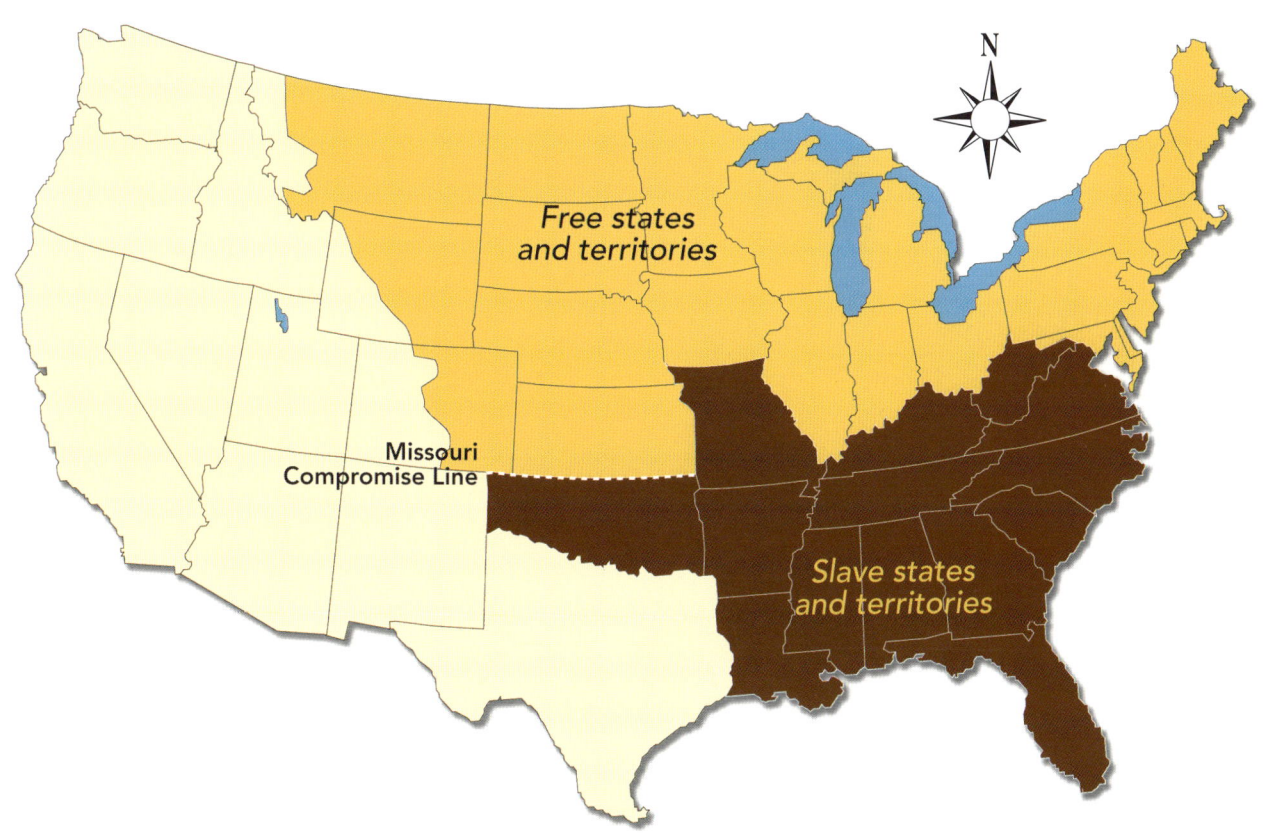

DRED SCOTT, THE SLAVE

With few records still in existence, some of Dred Scott's life is unknown. Facts such as his date of birth and his transfers from one owner to another vary among sources. Most sources agree that Dred was born in Southampton County, Virginia, sometime between 1795 and 1800. It is believed that the Peter Blow family owned Dred's parents. This meant that when Dred was born, he became the Blow family's property, too.

In 1819, Dred and the Blows' other slaves moved with the family to a cotton plantation in Alabama. On the plantation, the slaves planted, hoed, and picked cotton. Some sources indicate that this business failed. The Blows and their slaves then moved to St. Louis, Missouri, in 1830. There, Peter Blow ran a boarding house called the Jefferson Hotel. The Blow slaves worked in the boarding house cooking, cleaning, and doing odd jobs.

After working for the Blows, Dred was sold to a doctor named John Emerson. This sale occurred some time after the Blow family relocated to St. Louis in 1830 and before the end of 1833. Dred's price was reportedly $500. It is not clear whether Peter Blow sold Dred or if Blow's daughter, Elizabeth, sold Dred after her father's death in 1832.

Slaves picking cotton in a field

On October 25, 1833, Emerson was accepted into the U.S. Army as an assistant surgeon. Dred, who was close in age to Dr. Emerson, traveled with his new master to Fort Armstrong in Illinois that November. Slavery had been banned in the Illinois region since 1787. When Illinois became a state in 1818, the state constitution affirmed it as a free state. Yet Dred worked as a slave alongside his master at the fort.

Dr. Emerson soon requested a transfer from Fort Armstrong. Finally, in May 1836, Emerson got his wish. The U.S. War Department decided to close the fort. The fort's log buildings were old, rotted, and prone to leaking. In addition, army leaders doubted that the fort could protect people from the area's increasingly hostile Native American tribes.

From Fort Armstrong, Emerson and Scott moved to Fort Snelling in the newly created Wisconsin Territory. The fort was located near present-day St. Paul, Minnesota. Slavery had been banned in this area since 1820.

While living at Fort Snelling, Dred met Major Lawrence Taliaferro. Taliaferro was an Indian agent. As such, he represented the U.S. government to the Native Americans. Dred married one of Taliaferro's slaves, a woman named Harriet Robinson. Taliaferro was a justice of the peace and performed the wedding ceremony. He either sold or gave Harriet to Emerson after the marriage.

Meanwhile, Dr. Emerson repeatedly made requests to leave Fort Snelling. He was transferred to St. Louis, Missouri, on October 20, 1837. On the first part of his journey, he traveled south down the Mississippi by canoe. Then he boarded a steamboat, which took him to St. Louis. Because he had so little room in the canoe, he took few

DID YOU KNOW?

A view of Fort Snelling from the 1840s

FORT SNELLING

Fort Snelling played an important role in Dred Scott's life. But the fort also affected the lives of most people living on the Upper Mississippi River. The fort signaled an American presence on the frontier in the 1820s. Colonel Josiah Snelling oversaw the fort's construction on a bluff above the Mississippi River. The U.S. Army finished the fort in 1825. For many years, Native Americans and fur traders met at the fort. Nearby settlements became the cities of Minneapolis and St. Paul.

belongings with him. Among the possessions he left behind were Dred and Harriet. They were hired out to others until Dr. Emerson could have them sent to join him.

Almost immediately upon his arrival in St. Louis, Emerson was reassigned to Fort Jessup in the western part of Louisiana. On November 22, 1837, he arrived at the fort and quickly decided that it was even worse than Fort Snelling. He requested a transfer back to Fort Snelling.

During the months he lived in Louisiana, Emerson met and married Eliza Irene Sanford. People called her Irene. In April 1838, shortly after his marriage to Irene, Emerson sent for Dred and Harriet. They joined the Emersons in the slave state of Louisiana.

In September, Emerson received his transfer to Fort Snelling. That month, the Emersons and the Scotts spent a short time in St. Louis. Then they boarded a steamship to return to Fort Snelling. On the ship, Harriet gave birth to the first of the Scotts' two children. The Scotts named the girl Eliza. She was born in a free territory and named after Dr. Emerson's wife. All five arrived at Fort Snelling in October.

The Emersons and Scotts remained at Fort Snelling for about two years. In May 1840, Dr. Emerson was transferred to Florida. Irene Emerson brought the Scott family with her to St. Louis. There they lived with Irene's father, Alexander Sanford, on his plantation. The Scotts were hired out to other families during this time.

Dr. Emerson was honorably discharged from the U.S. Army in August 1842. After his discharge, Dr. Emerson was unable to maintain a medical practice in St. Louis. So he and his wife moved to the Iowa Territory. There, they settled on land he had purchased while in the army. While no records exist to confirm it, it is believed that the Scotts remained in St. Louis during this time and continued to be hired out.

On December 29, 1843, Dr. Emerson died. His will transferred ownership of the Scotts to his wife. Irene Emerson returned to St. Louis to live with her father. It is believed that the Scotts continued to live in St. Louis during this time. Irene Emerson hired them out to different people. Less than three years after the Scotts were willed to Irene Emerson, Dred and Harriet took legal steps to pursue their freedom.

Dred Scott   Harriet Scott

THE FIRST TRIAL

Dred Scott was about 50 years old when he and Harriet began the legal fight to win their freedom. Historians have wondered why Dred had waited so long to sue for his release from slavery. He hadn't taken advantage of opportunities for freedom as so many other slaves before him had.

Historians have noted three possible reasons for Dred's timing in pursuing his freedom. Some have suggested that Irene Emerson may have planned to sell Dred. Some think Dred may have just grown tired of being hired out to others. Other historians have suggested that perhaps Dred had offered to purchase freedom for himself and his family, but Irene refused the offer.

Whatever the reason, Dred and Harriet filed identical petitions on April 6, 1846, in the Missouri Circuit Court. They listed the free and slave states and territories in which they had lived, and they asked for the right to sue Irene Emerson for their freedom.

Slaves had the right to sue for their freedom in Missouri, thanks to an 1807 territorial statute. It was designed to protect people who were kept as slaves illegally. Each "freedom suit" filed by a slave included a request to sue for freedom, a charge against someone who had held the slave in false imprisonment, and testimony from witnesses.

20

A bronze plaque at the west gate of the Old Courthouse in St. Louis, Missouri, commemorates the trials of Dred and Harriet Scott. The first two of their trials took place in this courthouse.

The Emancipation Ordinance of Missouri eventually abolished slavery in the state in 1865.

Some freedom suits filed before Dred's paved the way for other slaves to sue for freedom. The 1824 *Winny v. Whitesides* freedom suit was one of those. It resulted in a Missouri Supreme Court decision in favor of the slave.

The 1787 Northwest Ordinance also affected the status of slaves. This federal law stated that slaves who lived in any American territory north and west of the Ohio River were to be freed even if they returned to a slave state.

The 1824 Missouri Supreme Court decision stated that any master who took his slave to a free territory or state had in effect freed that slave. This judicial reasoning was referred to as "once free, always free." Missouri judges who heard later freedom trials were to apply this reasoning to their decisions.

Between 1824 and 1844, many slaves used this law to sue for their freedom. Missouri's highest court ruled in favor of slaves many times in these cases. This time period became known as the golden age.

Dred and Harriet's right to sue was based on the years Dred had lived at Fort Armstrong in the free state of Illinois. They also based their case on the years they had both lived in Fort Snelling in the free territory of Wisconsin.

After a judge approved the Scotts' right to sue Irene Emerson, the two filed actions for assault and false imprisonment. They charged that their current master "beat, bruised and ill-treated" them. The action also accused Irene Emerson of holding Dred and Harriet in slavery when they should have been freed.

The Scotts' case went to trial on June 30, 1847. The trial took place in the St. Louis Courthouse. A lawyer named Samuel Mansfield Bay represented the Scotts. He had once been Missouri's attorney general as well as a state legislator.

A lawyer named George W. Goode represented Irene Emerson. He was from Virginia and strongly supported slavery. Alexander Hamilton was the lead judge in the case.

To win the case, the Scotts' lawyer had to prove two things. He had to show proof that the Scotts had lived in territories or states where slavery was illegal. Then he had to show that Dred and Harriet were held as slaves by Irene Emerson.

The Old Courthouse in St. Louis, Missouri, is famous for Dred Scott's trials in 1847 and 1850. Because of renovations in the 1850s, the courtroom where the trials occurred no longer exists.

To show that Dred and Harriet had once lived in free land, Bay produced witnesses who had known the Scotts at Fort Armstrong and Fort Snelling. This proved that they'd lived on free land.

To prove that Irene had held the Scotts as slaves, Bay called a number of witnesses. Henry Taylor Blow stated under oath that his father had sold Dred to John Emerson. People who had lived in the military forts with John Emerson were also called as witnesses. They swore they had hired the Scotts from Dr. Emerson.

Bay also called another witness, Samuel Russell, to testify that he had hired Harriet and Dred from Irene Emerson. Russell swore in court that he paid Irene's father, Alexander Sanford, for the slaves' work. This established Irene's ownership of the Scotts.

Irene's lawyer, Goode, had to disprove testimony that could hurt his client. Under Goode's questioning, Russell admitted that he had not actually hired the Scotts but his wife, Adeline, had. He knew only what his wife told him about her arrangement with the Scotts. So, the judge told jury members they couldn't use Russell's testimony. Without this proof, the fact that Irene Emerson owned the Scotts was not proven. The jury's decision was in Irene's favor. Irene was able to keep her slaves because no one had proven that she owned them!

The lawyer representing the Scotts immediately requested a new trial. Russell's testimony, which had harmed their case, had been a surprise to them. Bay insisted that he could prove that the Scotts were Irene Emerson's slaves.

THE SECOND TRIAL

On March 17, 1848, between the Scotts' first and second trials for freedom, the St. Louis County sheriff was put in charge of Dred and his family. His role was to hire them out and manage their earnings until their case was settled. The sheriff retained custody of the Scotts for nine years.

Irene Emerson moved to Springfield, Massachusetts, sometime between 1849 and 1850, when she married Dr. Calvin C. Chaffee. Chaffee, a strong opponent of slavery, had been elected to the U.S. Congress shortly after he married Irene.

In 1851, Charles Edmund LeBeaume, Peter Blow's brother-in-law, hired Dred and Harriet to work for him. He employed them for seven years.

After the first trial, the Scotts and Irene Emerson hired new lawyers. The Scotts hired Alexander P. Field and David N. Hall. Field was also involved in Illinois and Wisconsin politics. He was known for winning court cases. Irene's family hired lawyers Hugh A. Garland and Lyman D. Norris.

On December 2, 1847, Judge Hamilton ordered a retrial of Dred and Harriet's case. However, it took more than two years for their case to be heard. A number of factors contributed to the long delay.

Dred Scott

First, the case had been referred to the Missouri Supreme Court and then returned to the St. Louis Circuit Court. A heavy circuit court schedule pushed the hearing back twice. A major fire in St. Louis brought much of the city's business to a standstill. Then an outbreak of cholera in St. Louis caused further delay.

The second trial finally opened on January 12, 1850. It was held in the same St. Louis courtroom as the first trial. Alexander Hamilton was once again the lead judge in the case. In this trial, the Scotts' lawyers, Field and Hall, presented the previous testimony of those who had hired the Scotts from Dr. Emerson. Field then called Adeline Russell to the stand. She testified that she had hired the Scotts directly from Irene Emerson. This was vital to the Scotts' freedom case. The absence of this information had led to defeat in their first trial.

Garland and Norris presented Irene's case. They tried to prove that Irene did not err in hiring out the Scotts while they lived at the military forts. They claimed that the Emersons were operating under military law, not civil law. Only civil law banned slavery in the Wisconsin and Illinois territories. The lawyers argued that military law took priority over civil law. If they were correct, this would mean that Dred and Harriet were not entitled to their freedom.

The lawyers' argument regarding military law over civil law had been attempted in an 1837 Missouri Supreme Court case. It hadn't worked then, and it didn't stand in the Scotts' case either. With proof of Irene's ownership of the Scotts before them, a jury of 12 white men granted the two their freedom.

Emerson's lawyers, Garland and Norris, requested a new trial. Their request was denied. Then they made an appeal to the Missouri

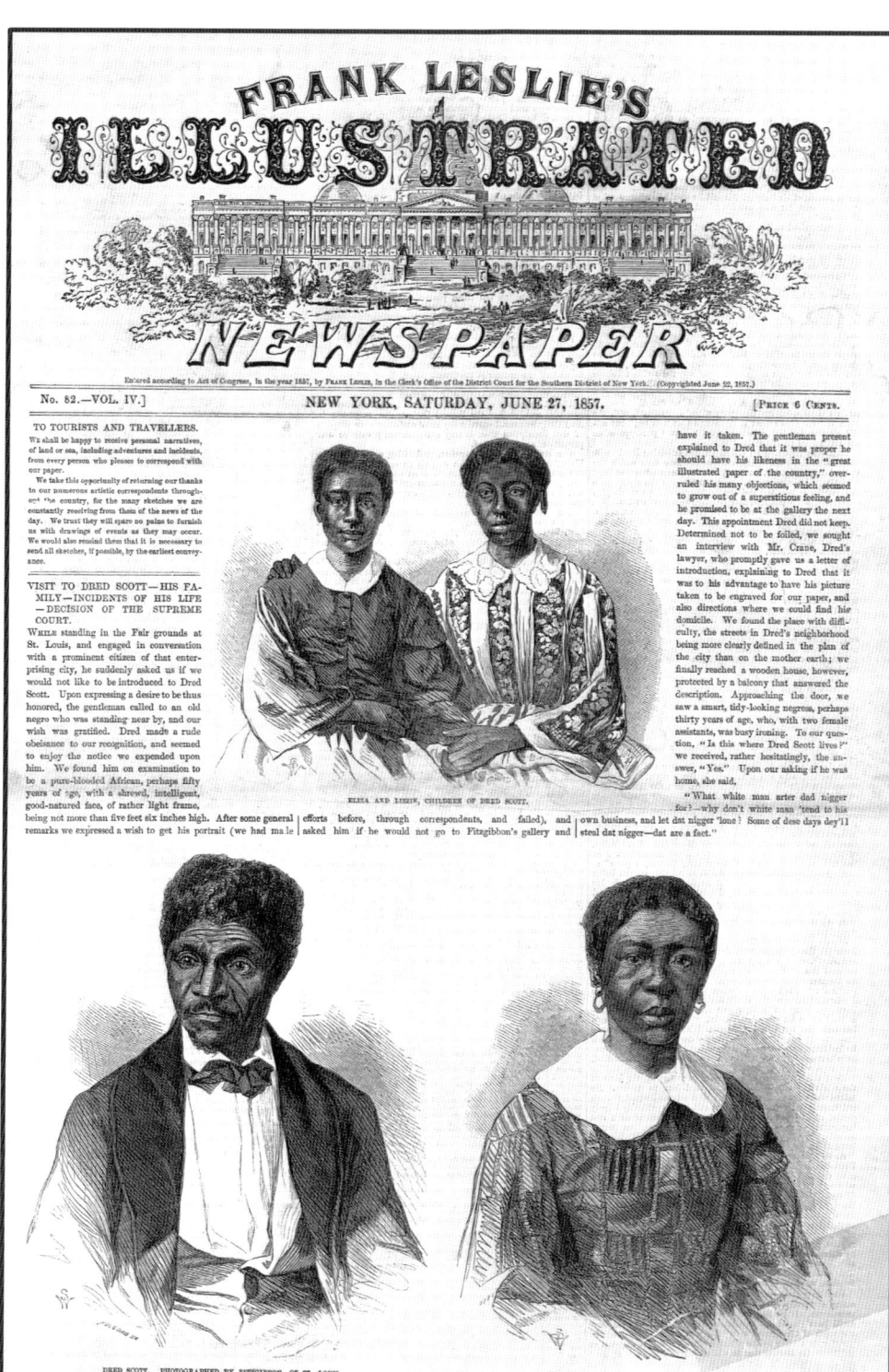

A copy of Frank Leslie's Illustrated Newspaper has a front page story on the Supreme Court's Dred Scott Decision of 1857. The story includes illustrations of Dred Scott and his family.

Supreme Court. Some historians believe that the justices of this court were waiting to take on a case such as this. Some have suggested that the Southern judges were eager to make a formal judicial stand in support of slavery. Garland and Norris's request was granted.

On February 12, 1850, attorneys for Dred and Harriet Scott and Irene Emerson all agreed that only the case of *Dred Scott v. Irene Emerson* would move forward. Whatever outcome resulted from that trial would apply to Harriet Scott's case, too.

That same year, the *Dred Scott v. Irene Emerson* case was heard in the Missouri Supreme Court. During the trial, elections forced two of the justices from their positions. The justices' summary opinion in the case had not been officially recorded when this happened. This meant that the case had to be retried.

The case came before the Missouri Supreme Court in the fall of 1851 to be reconsidered. Justices Hamilton Gamble, William Scott, and John Ryland heard the case. In the brief filed by Norris, he challenged the "once free, always free" reasoning for the first time. He questioned whether it was legally sound for the federal government to prohibit slavery in the territories.

Norris's challenge marked a turn in the Dred Scott case. The case was no longer about one slave using the court system to fight for his freedom. Dred's case had become a political tug-of-war. The case came to represent the South's pull for each state's right to control slavery versus the North's pull for the federal government to regulate slavery.

On March 22, 1852, Justice Gamble voted against the reversal. Justices Scott and Ryland voted in favor of reversing the circuit court's earlier decision. Justice Scott formally expressed his opinion regarding the case. He stated, "Every State has the right of

An antislavery meeting at Exeter Hall in New Hampshire

determining how far, in a spirit of comity {or observing other state's laws}, it will respect the laws of other States. Those laws have no intrinsic {or basic} right to be enforced beyond the limits of the State for which they have enacted. The respect allowed them will depend altogether on their conformity to the policy of our {Missouri} institutions. No State is bound to carry into effect enactments conceived in a spirit hostile to that which pervades her own laws."

Justice Scott's opinion meant that the Missouri courts did not feel obligated to abide by the laws of other states. For example, just because some states made slavery illegal, Missouri did not have to follow those laws. The judges' 2–1 vote meant that the rights of slave owners were upheld. Dred and Harriet were sent back into slavery.

FEDERAL COURT

On November 2, 1853, Dred filed a case against John Sanford, Irene's brother. Sanford had claimed ownership of the Scott family since Dred's second trial. Sanford had no paperwork to show any transfer of slave ownership. But Sanford had been assigned to manage Dr. Emerson's estate after the doctor's death. This may explain how Sanford came to see himself as the Scotts' owner.

Roswell M. Field replaced David Hall and Alexander Field as Dred's lawyer. Field took Dred's case without charging for his time. He eventually wanted to force the U.S. Supreme Court to settle one very important question: Were slaves entitled to permanent freedom if they had ever lived in a free state or territory? Lower courts had delivered conflicting answers to this question. Field wanted the highest court in the land to decide once and for all.

Before Dred's case went to the Supreme Court, it had to be decided by the U.S. Circuit Court for the District of Missouri. This federal court handled the case because the two parties in disagreement, the Scotts and John Sanford, lived in different states. The suit against Sanford sought freedom for both Dred and Harriet. It also sought to free the Scotts' daughters, Eliza and Lizzie. Dred also claimed that Emerson should pay $9,000 for damages.

In April 1854, Sanford's lawyer, Hugh Garland, challenged whether the court had the authority to hear Dred's case. Garland said

Many slave owners did not have proof of ownership because they acquired their slaves informally at slave auctions, such as the one shown here.

that because Dred was a "Negro of African descent," he was not a citizen of Missouri. His point was that if Dred were not a Missouri citizen, he would have no right to seek his freedom.

Judge Robert W. Wells heard both sides of the arguments. Wells said that while Dred was indeed not a true Missouri citizen, he did live in Missouri. This, the judge said, gave Dred the right to bring his case forward.

The lawyers on both sides prepared legal paperwork. It outlined Dred's life from the time he became Dr. Emerson's property through the 1852 Missouri Supreme Court decision that upheld Irene's right to own the Scotts.

A historian named Kenneth Kaufman suggested that this paperwork "signaled the point at which Dred Scott's freedom no longer depended on proving residence on free soil, but rather on proving that freedom, once gained on free soil, could be retained upon return to slave territory."

With no witnesses to call and no new information to introduce to the courts, the trial was brief. In May 1854, the circuit court jury decided in Sanford's favor. The Scotts were ordered to remain in slavery, under Sanford's ownership.

Dred's lawyer requested an appeal, but Judge Wells refused. Field filed the required paperwork to take Dred's case to the U.S. Supreme Court. Because there is no higher court in the United States, this marked Dred's final legal plea for freedom. To increase Dred's chance of winning his case, Field put Montgomery Blair in charge. Blair was an experienced and influential lawyer known for opposing slavery. John Sanford was also represented by well-qualified lawyers Henry S. Geyer and Reverdy Johnson.

The case of *Dred Scott v. Sandford* finally reached the Supreme Court on December 30, 1854. Sanford's name was spelled incorrectly on the court documents.

Earlier that same year, Congress had passed the Kansas-Nebraska Act. This act defined boundaries for the two newly created territories. It also allowed each territory to decide whether it would allow slavery or ban it. The Northerners were furious about the act's impact on the spread of slavery. The Southerners strongly supported this loosening of slavery prohibitions and the strengthening of states' rights.

By the time Dred's case was finally heard by the Supreme Court in February 1856, heightened tension brewed between the North and South. In Blair's summary of the case, he argued that Dred became free when he lived in the free state of Illinois with Dr. Emerson. He also argued that Dred should have retained his freedom even after returning to a slave state based on the legal standard of "once free, always free."

Blair also raised an issue he thought Sanford's lawyers would discuss. He questioned whether a "Negro of African descent" was a citizen of the United States. He stated that though Dred did not have the full rights of a U.S. citizen, he did at least have the right to sue for his freedom in the U.S. court system.

The U.S. Supreme Court building

Lawyers Johnson and Geyer challenged the federal government's right to create the Missouri Compromise of 1820. They also dismissed Missouri's obligation to abide by the terms of the Northwest Ordinance of 1787. If both of these federal laws were ignored, then Dred would never have been a free man. Johnson and Geyer argued exactly that and said Dred did not have the right to be free.

After each side made its argument, the nine justices met to discuss the case. They failed to reach a decision. On May 12, the Court ordered that the case be argued again.

When Dred's case was heard again that December, George Ticknor Curtis helped Blair argue the case on Dred's behalf. He was a constitutional lawyer from Boston whose brother, Benjamin Curtis, was one of the U.S. Supreme Court justices hearing Dred's case. George Ticknor Curtis was especially knowledgeable about the power Congress had in dealing with slavery in the territories.

Chief Justice Roger B. Taney

The courtroom was packed on March 6, 1857. All anxiously awaited Chief Justice Roger B. Taney's summary of Dred's case. His summary represented what the majority of the Supreme Court justices had decided.

Regarding whether Dred Scott was a citizen, Taney said no. He stated that the authors of the Declaration of Independence had not planned to include black people when they wrote, "all men are created equal." Taney was saying, in effect, that Dred had no right to file a suit in a federal court.

Next, Taney addressed the issue of whether or not Dred was free because he had lived in a territory where slavery was made illegal by the Missouri Compromise. Taney wrote that he was not. Taney explained that the Missouri Compromise of 1820 was unconstitutional. He said that the U.S. Constitution had guaranteed citizens the right to own property. Slaves were considered property. The federal government had no right, Taney said, to restrict where slave owners could take their slaves.

Regarding the question of Dred's right to freedom because he had lived in the free state of Illinois, Taney said no. He said that Illinois laws did not apply in Missouri. Once Dred returned to Missouri, he became a slave again under Missouri law.

Taney went on to say that African Americans were "beings of an inferior order . . . so far inferior, that they had no rights which the white man was bound to respect." Taney returned the case to the circuit court. He instructed the court to dismiss it. What the court dismissed, most Northerners could not.

AFTER THE SUPREME COURT DECISION

The Supreme Court majority opinion set off a firestorm of controversy. Justice Curtis opposed the decision. He resigned from his position because of his disappointment in the ruling.

The Supreme Court ruling, of course, excited Southerners. They were pleased that the Missouri Compromise could no longer dictate where slave owners could take their slaves. The *Constitutionalist* newspaper boasted, "Southern opinion upon the subject of slavery . . . is now the law of the land."

In the North, newspapers exclaimed disgust over the Supreme Court ruling. Horace Greeley, an abolitionist and editor of the *New York Tribune,* called the Supreme Court's decision, "atrocious, wicked, and abominable." Some Northerners believed that the Southerners were working to make slavery legal across the United States. Many gathered at town meetings to express their anger.

Days after the Supreme Court decision was made public, the Springfield, Massachusetts's newspaper *Argus* published new information about the case. It stated that Irene Emerson's second husband, Calvin Chaffee, actually had ownership of Dred Scott.

Many Northerners wondered how a Republican abolitionist and congressman could own slaves.

Chaffee explained that he did not know that Irene's first husband had owned Dred Scott until February 1857. He declared that he had nothing to do with the case. He said that his own lawyer had advised him to say nothing about the case until a decision was reached.

On May 26, 1857, Chaffee and his family gave all legal rights to the Scotts to Henry Taylor Blow. He was Peter Blow's son and Dred's longtime friend. Blow accompanied Dred and Harriet to the Missouri Circuit Court that same day. Judge Alexander Hamilton granted the Scotts their freedom. Though Dred's fight for freedom had dragged on for more than 11 years, he was only able to enjoy his freedom for just over one year. Dred died of a lung disease called tuberculosis on September 17, 1858.

African Americans in Washington DC celebrate the fourth anniversary of the District of Columbia's Emancipation Act. In 1862, the act ended slavery in the nation's capital.

American Moments

THE EFFECT OF DRED'S CASE

Chief Justice Taney may have thought the Court's majority decision would protect the institution of slavery. It did just the opposite. The Dred Scott decision pushed those against slavery to gain control of the U.S. Congress. Taney and several other Supreme Court justices were nearing 80 years old. Northerners believed that if they voted for a Republican president, he would nominate replacement judges who were against slavery.

With a majority of Northerners voting for him, Republican Abraham Lincoln was elected president of the United States in 1860. Lincoln clearly represented the opinions of those in the North who opposed slavery.

Barely one month after Lincoln's election, South Carolina withdrew from the Union in protest. Soon six more Southern states followed South Carolina's lead. These states wanted to form their own nation, one that would protect the rights of slave owners. They formed the Confederate States of America.

Abraham Lincoln

Lincoln was determined to keep the nation united. Instead, fighting broke out between the North and the South. The Civil War began in 1861, and four more Southern states joined the Confederacy. What began as a fight over states' rights versus the federal government's rights became a moral war over slavery. Not until the North's victory in 1865 did the bloody conflict end.

Later that year, the Thirteenth Amendment to the Constitution abolished slavery. Some believed the amendment was needed because the Emancipation Proclamation might be found to be unconstitutional.

In 1868, Congress passed the Fourteenth Amendment to the Constitution. It declared that all people born or naturalized in the United States, including Negroes, shared all citizenship benefits equally.

Legal historians have labeled the Dred Scott decision a "ghastly error." Yet, Dred Scott's freedom suit elevated the slavery debate to the U.S. Supreme Court. Though Dred Scott's freedom was short-lived, his case helped ensure lasting freedom for African Americans after him.

EMANCIPATION PROCLAMATION

On September 22, 1862, President Abraham Lincoln issued a preliminary Emancipation Proclamation. The proclamation declared that on January 1, 1863, all slaves in the Confederacy would be free. No slaves were actually freed by the proclamation, but the declaration was an important step in the eventual elimination of slavery.

Lincoln liberating a slave

TIMELINE

1795 to 1800 — Dred Scott is born into slavery in Virginia.

1803 — The Louisiana Purchase doubles the size of the United States.

1820 — The U.S. Congress agrees to the Missouri Compromise. The compromise allows Missouri to enter the Union as a slave state.

1830 to 1833 — Dr. John Emerson purchases Dred Scott. The exact date of the purchase is unknown.

1843 — Dr. Emerson dies. Emerson's wife, Irene, inherits Dred Scott.

1846 — Dred Scott and his wife, Harriet, sue Irene Emerson for their freedom.

1847 — The Scotts' case goes to trial, they lose, but the judge orders a retrial.

1850 — Dred and Harriet's second trial begins.

1852 — The Missouri Supreme Court rules against Dred and Harriet. The Scotts return to slavery.

1853 — Dred sues again for freedom.

1857 — The U.S. Supreme Court denies Dred Scott his freedom.

The Scotts' owner, Henry Taylor Blow, gives Dred and Harriet their freedom.

1858 — Dred Scott dies.

1861 to 1865 — The Union and Confederacy fight the Civil War.

1865 — The Thirteenth Amendment ends slavery in United States.

1868 — The Fourteenth Amendment to the Constitution is ratified. The amendment protects the rights of all U.S. citizens, including African Americans.

American Moments

FAST FACTS

Slaves' births and deaths were typically not recorded, so the specific date of Dred's birth is not currently known.

Former slaves sometimes published accounts of their bondage. These accounts, called slave narratives, were popular during the years of Dred Scott's court actions. Slave narratives sold thousands of copies and were translated into many languages.

The Kansas-Nebraska Act of 1854 led to violence between antislavery and proslavery settlers in Kansas. Settlers fought each other to determine whether Kansas would be slave territory or free territory. Kansas became a free state in 1861.

The Fugitive Slave Act of 1850 caused further tensions between Northern and Southern states. The act said U.S. citizens had to help recover fugitive slaves. Both fugitive and free African Americans were captured and taken to slave states. Abolitionists were outraged by the law.

After 1852, few slaves in Missouri won their freedom through the courts.

During Dred Scott's lifetime, many free African Americans lived in St. Louis, Missouri.

After receiving his freedom, Dred Scott worked as a porter at a hotel in St. Louis, Missouri.

WEB SITES
WWW.ABDOPUB.COM

Would you like to learn more about the Dred Scott Decision? Please visit **www.abdopub.com** to find up-to-date Web site links about the Dred Scott Decision and other American moments. These links are routinely monitored and updated to provide the most current information available.

Slaves celebrate their newfound freedom.

GLOSSARY

abolitionist: someone who is against slavery.

appeal: to ask a higher court to review the decision of a lower court.

attorney general: the chief law officer of a national or state government.

bondage: the state of being under another person's control.

brief: a formal outline that lists the main points of a lawyer's argument. It includes supporting evidence.

circuit court: a state court.

cholera: an intestinal disease characterized by vomiting and diarrhea.

Confederacy: the country formed by the states of South Carolina, Georgia, Florida, Alabama, Louisiana, Mississippi, Texas, Virginia, Tennessee, Arkansas, and North Carolina that left the Union between 1860 and 1861.

indigo: a shrub with leaves that can be used to produce a deep blue dye.

justice: a judge on a state supreme court or the U.S. Supreme Court.

naturalize: to make a foreign-born person a citizen.

petition: to make a formal request to a person of authority.

plea: an earnest request.

statute: a law made by the legislative branch of the government.

testimony: what is said in a court of law while under oath.

Union: the states that remained in the United States during the Civil War.

INDEX

B
Bay, Samuel Mansfield 23, 25
Blair, Montgomery 34–36
Blow, Elizabeth 14
Blow, Henry Taylor 25, 39
Blow, Peter 14, 26, 39

C
Chaffee, Calvin C. 26, 38, 39
Civil War, U.S. 41
Clay, Henry 12
Congress, U.S. 7, 12, 36, 41
Curtis, Benjamin 36, 38
Curtis, George Ticknor 36

D
Declaration of Independence 37

E
Emerson, Eliza Irene Sanford 18–20, 23, 25, 26, 28, 30, 32, 38
Emerson, John 14, 16, 18, 19, 25, 28, 32, 33, 35, 39

F
Field, Alexander P. 26, 28, 32
Field, Roswell M. 32, 34
Fort Armstrong 16, 23, 25
Fort Jessup 18
Fort Snelling 16, 18, 23, 25
Fourteenth Amendment 41

G
Gamble, Hamilton 30
Garland, Hugh A. 26, 28, 30, 32
Geyer, Henry S. 34, 36
Goode, George W. 23, 25

H
Hall, David N. 26, 28, 32
Hamilton, Alexander 23, 25, 26, 28, 39

J
Jamestown, Virginia 4
Johnson, Reverdy 34, 36

K
Kansas-Nebraska Act 34

L
LeBeaume, Charles Edmund 26
Lincoln, Abraham 40, 41
Louisiana Purchase 11

M
Missouri Circuit Court 4, 20, 39
Missouri Compromise 12, 13, 36–38
Missouri Supreme Court 22, 23, 28, 30, 33

N
Norris, Lyman D. 26, 28, 30
Northwest Ordinance 7, 22, 36

R
Russell, Adeline 25, 28
Russell, Samuel 25
Ryland, John 30

S
Sanford, Alexander 18, 25
Sanford, John 32, 34, 35
Scott, Eliza 18, 32
Scott, Harriet Robinson 4, 16, 18–20, 23, 25, 26, 28, 30, 31, 32–34, 39
Scott, Lizzie 32
Scott, William 30, 31
Supreme Court, U.S. 32, 34–38, 40

T
Taliaferro, Lawrence 16
Taney, Roger B. 37, 40
Thirteenth Amendment 41

W
Wells, Robert W. 33, 34
Whitney, Eli 10